Life After Whale

Life After Whale

THE AMAZING ECOSYSTEM OF A WHALE FALL

Lynn Brunelle

Illustrations by
Jason Chin

NEAL PORTER BOOKS
HOLIDAY HOUSE / NEW YORK

She drifts slowly. The late afternoon
sunlight slants through the rippled
water overhead and streams down
the skin on her back.

Just above her, thousands of tiny, shrimp-like krill merge and mingle into a massive pink cloud near the surface. With a single beat of her enormous tail fluke, she surges upward and . . .

lunges!

Her jaws close, trapping countless krill in her mouth while her elephant-sized tongue shoves around 21,000 gallons of seawater out through the baleen, a kind of filter attached to her upper jaw. The baleen is thin enough to let the water flow through and thick enough to capture the tiny crustaceans. In one hefty gulp, she swallows enough krill to fill a school bus.

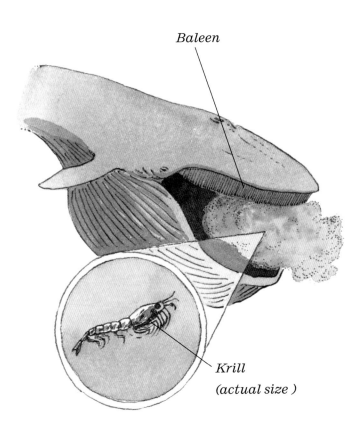

Baleen

Krill
(actual size)

She is a blue whale—the largest animal ever seen on Earth. This beautiful creature measures over 85 feet long—and would be more than eight stories tall if she walked on land. She would dwarf any dinosaur. And yet she moves with grace and power, like a dancer, as she plunges, drifts, and whirls above and below the currents of the Pacific Ocean.

Blue Whale: up to 110 ft long / up to 165 tons

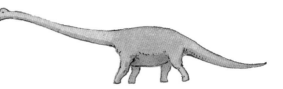

Titanosaur: 85 ft long / 65 tons

African Elephant: 10 ft at shoulder / 5 tons

Human Child: 4 ft at shoulder / 50 pounds

Her years are told in her ears.

Every six months a new layer of wax lines her ear canal. In summer, when there is much to eat, the layer is light colored; and in winter, when there is less food, the color is darker. Like rings in a tree trunk, these layers tell her age. One hundred and eighty rings line each of her ears.

The rings can tell so much more. Chemical stories that whisper about the history of the oceans, the temperatures of the water, or the pollution in the sea. They can show how many times she was pregnant, whether or not the feeding was good in a certain summer, or if the travel each spring or fall was hard or not.

They are rings that measure a lifetime.

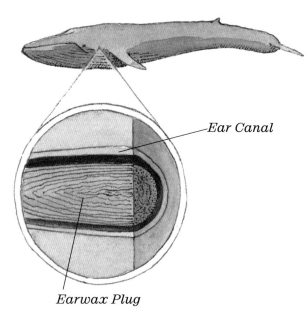

Ear Canal

Earwax Plug

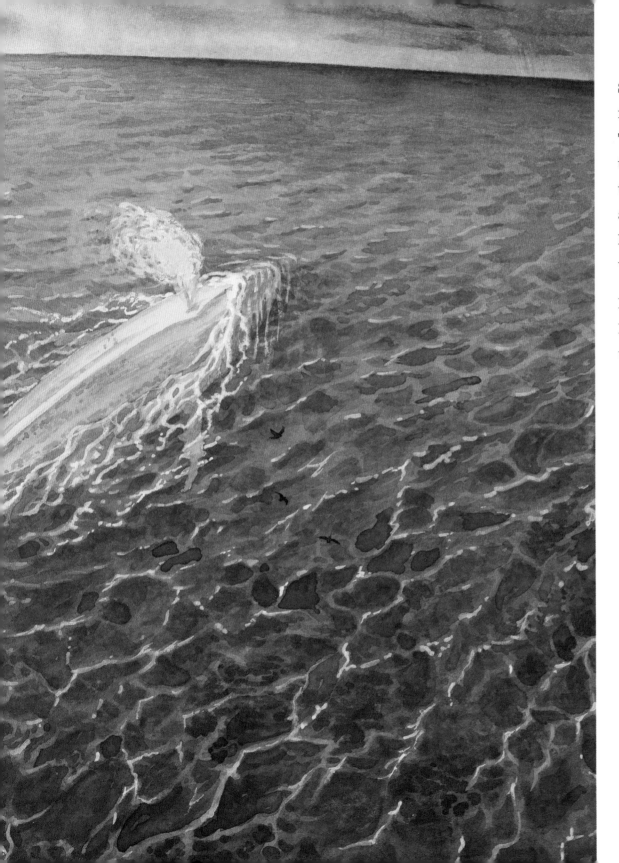

She has spent her years on the planet moving from the northern chill to the tropical warmth. This is her ninetieth trip northward. As she travels, she sends a long, single-note humming tone out into the deep sea by pushing air around the spaces in her head. Her calls are louder than a jet engine and are heard by other whales over 500 miles away.

Her 400-pound heart is the size of a golf cart. It has never failed to push blood and oxygen to every cell of her enormous body.

North Pacific
Blue Whale Range

Summer

Winter

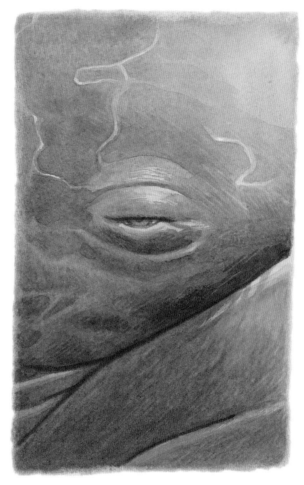

But today something is different. Her heart is slowing down. It is wearing out. It is pumping less and less oxygen to her lungs, brain, and other internal organs. This year she will not make it to the feeding waters in the north.

Her vision blurs and darkens. Her breathing slows. Her awareness fades. Her heart quiets and finally stops.

This year, this day, this moment, after ninety years of life, as all living things must do at some point . . .

she dies.

It is the end of one story—the story of a whale's life. But it is just the beginning of another story.

The death of a whale awakens and ignites a cascade of new life.

An entirely new ecosystem will build around this singular whale's passing. Her body will provide shelter and food for millions of creatures for more than a hundred years. A whole new world will arise. Scientists call this a whale fall.

It starts right away.

Gases begin to expand in the whale's body and it floats up to the surface of the ocean. Bacteria, which have lived harmlessly within the whale her whole life, are no longer being controlled by her immune system, and they grow wildly. They begin breaking down cells and creating more gases. The heat of the sun warms the body and chemicals leach out into the water, signaling to scavengers that food is available.

Sharks and fish zip to the scene and begin to nibble at the part of the whale that is underwater, while seabirds fly in and feast from above. As time passes, gases such as carbon dioxide and methane leak out and scatter into the surrounding air and water. The body is no longer kept afloat and it starts to sink.

For the first few feet, the water is bright blue and warm. Sunlight pierces the surface and lights up the top layer.

But the sun can only reach so far, and as the whale body falls through the bright blue layer into the darker, inky-colored water, the temperature plummets.

The weight of the water is colossal. As the whale body sinks, the pressure squashes in and squeezes the air out of the sinuses, lungs, and inner ear. Bubbles escape and rise from the body, twinkling silver in the sunlight just before they pop through the surface.

The body keeps falling through quiet stillness. Sometimes only inches per hour, sometimes yards, depending on the level of saltiness or temperature or current in the surrounding water.

Glowing shrimp, jellyfish, and other creatures twinkle nearby in the dark. A 130-foot long, wormlike siphonophore wiggles and flashes like a bizarre string of holiday lights. A bloody-belly comb jelly flickers with eight rows of glittering-rainbow light pathways that rim its bright red body. In the distance, a barreleye fish floats by with two glowing green globe eyes set in a see-through head.

These sparkles of light are called bioluminescence, created within the bodies of creatures when chemical reactions inside cells give off light. A shimmering language is sent out to communicate across the sunless seawater. Green and blue trails flash and streak as the whale sinks past.

Days pass. The whale body drops deeper and deeper. The sparkling in the surrounding water is less frequent as fewer and fewer creatures can survive at these depths.

At 3,000 feet below the surface, the whale body slips out of reach of the sun's longest rays.

The dark blue of the sea makes an almost imperceptible shift to pure black.

For almost a month more, the whale body slides downward through the frigid, pitch-black water. Eventually it lands softly on the seafloor over 6,000 feet (more than a mile) down, kicking up a tiny cloud of what looks like snow. It's called marine snow, but it's actually microscopic bits of dead animals and plants and minuscule skeletons of diatoms (tiny algae that live in the sea). Marine snow drifts down to rest for thousands, even millions, of years on the lightless seafloor—undisturbed . . . until now.

It is hard to sustain life in this barren place. The temperature of the water hovers around freezing, and the pressure of all the water overhead is crushing. There is no light, and food is scarce. Most creatures, such as vampire squids, squat lobsters, and eel larvae, survive by eating marine snow. It does not contain a lot of nutrition, but it's enough to keep a few resourceful creatures alive.

So when hundreds of thousands of pounds of food falls from above all at once, things change.

Generations and generations of over four hundred different species of deep-sea creatures, from fish to worms to crabs, clams, jellies, eels, and octopuses, will feed, grow, have babies, and thrive on the body of this whale. Other creatures will feed on the animals feeding on the whale.

The whale body becomes the foundation for an ecosystem tangled with food chains and webs, interlocking the lives of thousands of creatures.

Scientists look at the timelines of whale fall ecosystems in terms of overlapping phases.

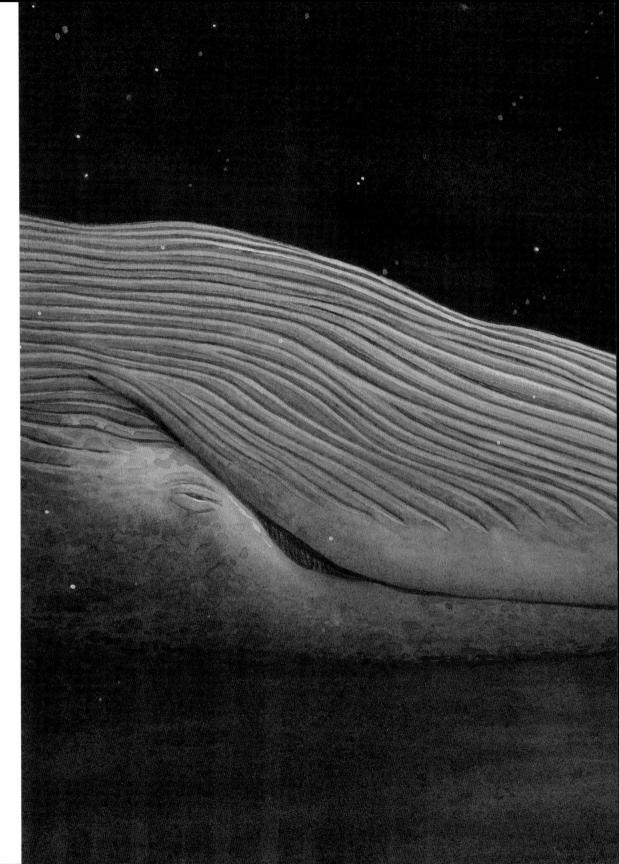

The first phase is known as the **mobile scavenger phase**. In this phase animals eat the muscle and fat tissue, leaving behind the skeleton.

When a carcass lands at the bottom of the sea, it gives off a trail of chemicals that reaches across miles of open water. Hungry scavengers will emerge from the darkness almost immediately.

A pink, eel-like hagfish is first on the scene. It ripples like a ribbon through the water, searching for food.

It has picked up the scent of molecules emitted by the whale's body. The hagfish zeroes in, follows the trail to the whale, and slams its head, face-first, into the soft flesh.

Hagfish do not have jaws like other fish. Their mouths are round suckers lined with two rows of sharp, scaly teeth. It tunnels deep and begins to feed, sucking up nutrients through its mouth and through its slimy pink skin.

More and more hagfish descend on the whale. Their feeding sends more food chemicals into the water, alerting more scavengers. The frenzy also invites predator fish that may be looking to make a meal of a hagfish.

This, however, is not as easy as it may seem. A fish that tries to take a bite of a hagfish gets a nasty surprise. When a hagfish is harassed, it instantly blasts bucket-loads of slime out of the tiny pores on its skin. The gooey mucus cloud clogs the mouth and gills of any would-be predator and sends it off gagging as the hagfish continues to eat, unharmed.

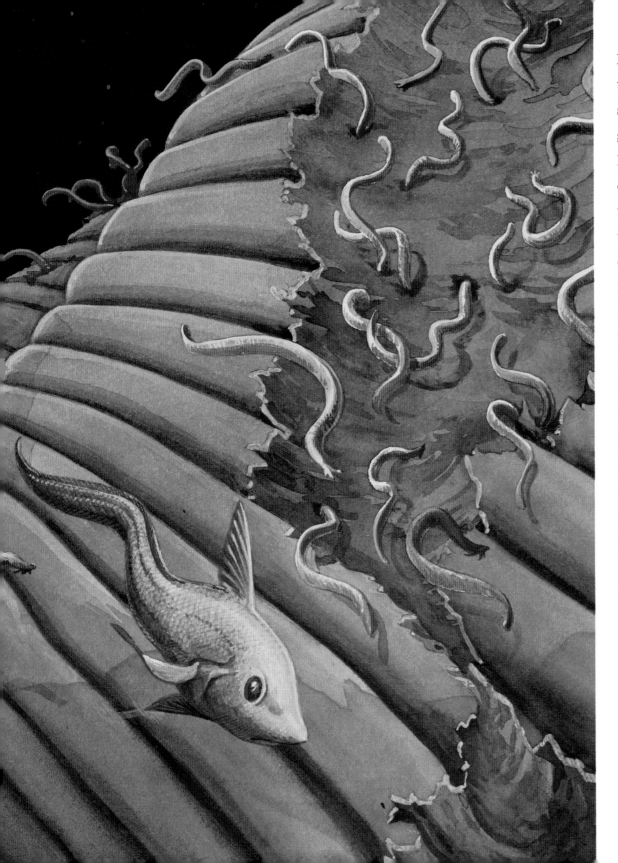

Moving like a silent, 22-foot-long, food-seeking torpedo, a sleeper shark zooms in. This deep-sea eating machine is built for finding and gobbling up things that fall to the seafloor. Practically blind, the sleeper shark's small eyes do not see very well in the dark, but the shark's smelling skills more than make up for that. Like the hagfish, it can sense chemicals in the water over a mile away and make a beeline to a fresh whale fall. It has a powerful bite with rows of razor-sharp teeth—perfect for chomping off huge chunks of meat.

Grenadiers, also known as rattail fish, arrive soon after the sleeper sharks and strip away flesh with their knife-like teeth. They are sloppy eaters, spewing out chunks of whale flesh as they chew. These irresistible tidbits scatter the surrounding seafloor and lure even more hungry animals.

The first food chains are beginning.

Rattail

Eelpout

King Crab

After a few weeks pass, the carcass is a busy city. It crawls with squat lobsters that scooch across the surface, pinch off hunks of flesh, and stuff themselves.

Millions of sea scuds scamper across the skeleton and pick it clean.

Octopuses nestle into the ribcage and devour the soft tissue and cartilage in between bones.

Like guests that gorge themselves at an all-you-can-eat buffet, these creatures will doze as they rest between feedings.

Even though together these scavengers can eat 80 pounds of whale blubber and muscle every day, it still takes years to finish off the soft flesh of a whale.

Muusoctopus

Sea Scud

Blob Sculpin

Squat Lobster

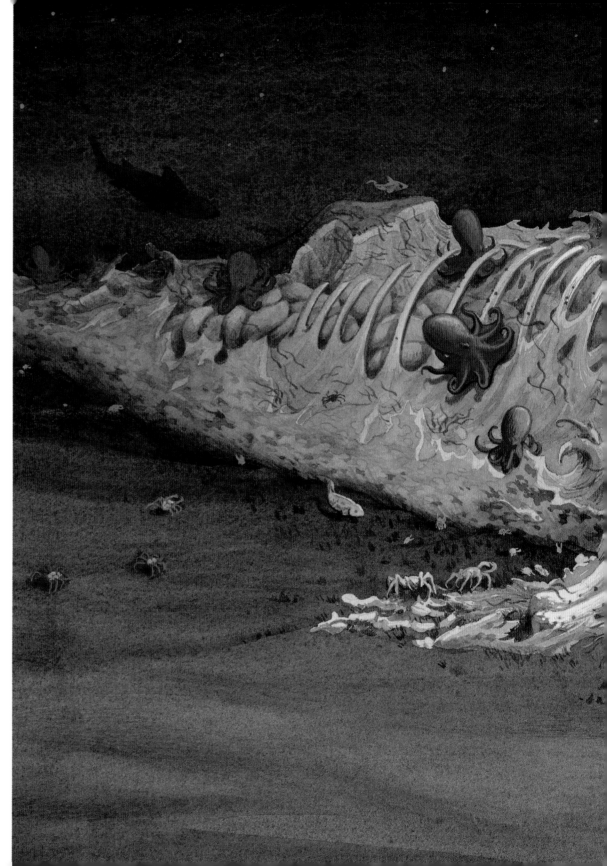

After the skeleton is picked clean and the bones are exposed, there is still plenty of food to be had by the next group of deep-sea diners. A new phase of life at a whale fall starts.

Phase two is known as the **enrichment opportunist phase**. For up to two years, a new wave of creatures arrives to take advantage of the leftovers from the original scavengers. Fragments of decomposing flesh and waste material enrich the sediment around the carcass. Crabs, snails, clams, and worms are the opportunists. They discover the remains, plunge themselves into the mud surrounding the skeleton, and feed on the scraps left behind. As days, weeks, and months pass, colonies of clams, snails, and crabs grow, expand, and cover the area around the skeleton.

Brittle Star

Snail

Sea Cucumber

Tube Worms

Floating freely through the ocean are countless microscopic worm larvae, carrying a team of bacteria waiting for the right opportunity to grow and flourish. The bacteria help the worms to feed, and the worms give the bacteria a safe place to live. Most of the larvae are eaten up by other sea creatures, but some get lucky.

The larva of a bone-eating zombie worm alights on a rib and sends out tiny roots that slowly squeeze their way into the bone. Inside the roots, the bacteria create an acid, which seeps into the whale bone and begins to dissolve it. This frees up fats and other chemicals for the worms and the bacteria to devour and digest. It also creates a space in the bone where the roots wedge in. Eventually the worm is firmly attached and feeding.

This worm has no eyes, stomach, or even a mouth. A feathery red body sprouts up and waves gently in the water, soaking up oxygen and releasing thousands and thousands of eggs loaded with their helpful bacteria. The eggs hatch into larvae, which float and settle on nearby bones, develop, and root in.

In time the skeleton looks as if it has a new coat of glowing pink fur. Each strand is a worm. These small scavengers can spend as long as ten years harvesting the food locked within the bones of the whale. And those bones, both big and small, begin to crumble away.

Years pass. Life on the whale fall is still changing. The flurry of activity is mostly microscopic now.

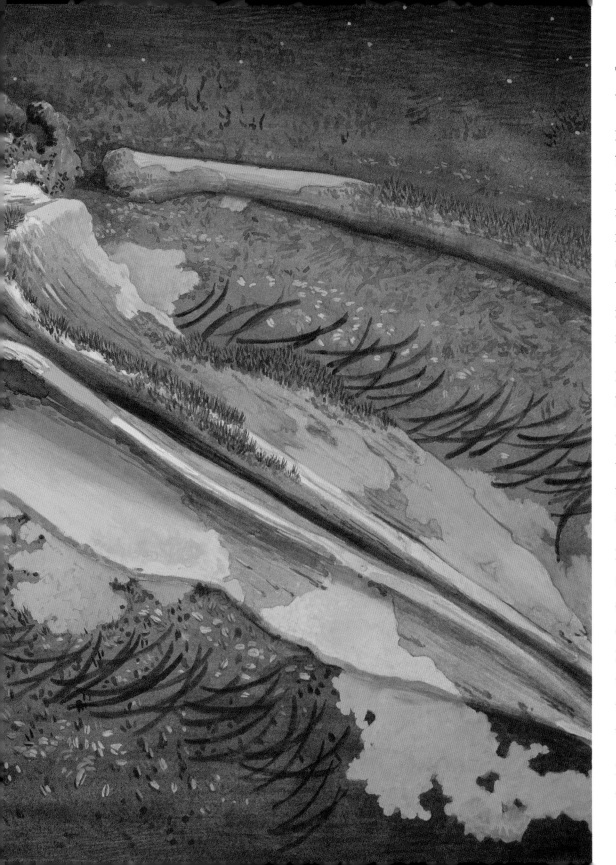

This phase is called the **sulfophilic phase**. It will last over a century.

Drawn to the chemicals released by the worms, blankets of bacteria in vibrant oranges, yellows, reds, and whites cover every inch of the remaining skeleton. They break down the fats inside the cells, use up oxygen, and create sulfur-rich chemicals like hydrogen sulfide. With a rotten-egg smell, these chemicals leak into the water and, in turn, advertise a new menu.

Hydrogen sulfide is poisonous to many life-forms, but to some deep-sea creatures it's a banquet.

Rare species of hungry snails, mussels, and worms, their guts souped-up with swarms of their own sulfur-loving bacteria, creep, wriggle, and float in to graze.

Resourceful clams bury themselves in the surrounding mud. They may look like regular clams at first glance, but they are very different under the shell. They have no gut. Instead, they contain mostly red, fluffy gills that store specific bacteria inside that allow them to turn sulfur into sugar, which fuels the clam.

By now, the whale's body has created one of the biggest ecosystems on the seafloor!

Over one hundred and fifty years have passed since the whale fell to the seafloor. The hard structure of the bones still stands. These giant bones offer a place to live and a boost up into the currents near the ocean floor. Being higher in the water allows filter-feeding animals, such as sponges and anemones, a better place to screen the water for falling marine snow.

This stage is called the **reef phase**, and it overlaps with the **sulfophilic phase**. While the large bones reach upward, chemicals such as calcium, nitrates, and phosphates seep from them and mingle with the water, but they don't stay in the deep forever.

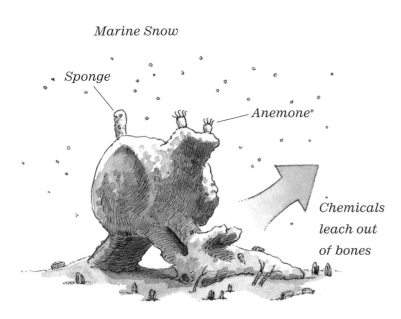

Marine Snow

Sponge

Anemone

Chemicals leach out of bones

Every spring, cool, dense water rises up toward the ocean surface carrying nutrients from the deep with it. This year, it contains chemicals from the whale fall, too. When the nutrients rise to the upper layers, where the sun's rays light up and warm the waters, they feed massive blooms of algae and other plankton, which in turn feed krill.

Sunlight shimmers down and the water is full of life. Clouds of krill swarm together, a whirl of energy as they dine on the abundant plankton. They are not aware of the huge, gaping mouth that looms up from beneath to devour them.

Upwelling

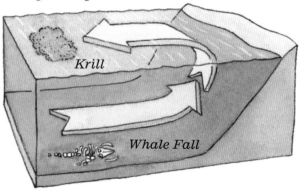

Krill

Whale Fall

Beginning in spring every year, winds blowing along the west coast of the United States cause surface water to move away from the shore. When this warmer water moves out to sea, cold water from the deep rises up to replace it, like a massive conveyor belt. This process is called upwelling. The cold water is rich in chemical nutrients that fertilize phytoplankton (algae and other photosynthesizing plankton) near the surface. Phytoplankton are critical to the ocean food web, feeding krill and many other species.

A hungry young blue whale surges, scoops, and strains the water through her long baleen, feasting on the krill.

She gives her tail fluke a beat and swallows a busload-sized mouthful of tiny krill. Krill that have been fed by the plankton that were fattened on the nutrients gleaned from the remains of a long-gone whale.

She carries a calf inside her, which she will give birth to in the wintertime when she returns to warmer southern waters.

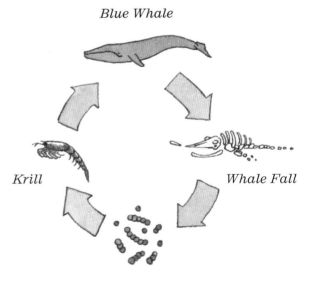

Blue Whale

Krill

Whale Fall

Phytoplankton

And, in a beautiful, circular way, the whales
of the past, the present, and the future swim on.

A Bit About Blue Whales

Blue whales can be found in all the oceans except the Arctic Ocean. They generally feed in polar waters and then migrate to warmer waters around the equator to breed and give birth. Whales are not fish. They are mammals. They breathe air, are warm-blooded, and feed their babies with milk from their mothers.

Blue whales are the biggest animals to have ever lived on Earth. Three school buses long and fifteen school buses heavy, blue whales are bigger than any land animal that ever was—-including dinosaurs. Blue whales can be so enormous because they live in the sea and the water supports their bodies. On land, skeletons can't support huge, heavy bodies because gravity is always pulling on them. But in the water, gravity is not an issue and huge bodies have more support.

A whale's nose is on top of its head. It's called the blowhole. When a blue whale exhales through its blowhole, the watery outbreath can blow 30 feet high.

Blue whales are filter feeders. They eat massive amounts of tiny animals called krill—up to sixteen tons a day. The whale's throat is pleated so it can expand and hold more water than the weight of the whale itself. The huge tongue pushes out the water through the baleen. Eight hundred thin plates of baleen grow down from the gums of the whale's upper jaw like a Venetian blind. Baleen is made of keratin—the same material that makes up your fingernails. Each 3-foot long plate has bristly edges that weave together to form a kind of mat for trapping the krill. Some species of snails make their home within the bristly baleen fibers!

The grooves on the throat of a blue whale act like an accordion—opening up and expanding so the whale's mouth can hold around 21,000 gallons of water and food.

Whales push air through big spaces in their sinuses to make deep, low-frequency sounds that can travel hundreds of miles! They are some of the loudest animals on the planet, and our ears can't even hear the lowest frequencies. The sounds are between 10 and 40 hertz and human ears can't pick up vibrations lower than 20 hertz. Both male and female blue whales make sounds, or vocalizations, but only males repeat sounds in a recognizable pattern that scientists recognize as "songs." Want to hear a blue whale sing? Check out this website from the Pacific Life Foundation: https://voicesinthesea.ucsd.edu/species/baleenWhales/blue.html

When a baby blue whale is born, it is the size of an elephant and grows 200 pounds a day. It lives off its mother's milk and grows 50 feet in six months. When it is six months old it has developed baleen plates and can start eating krill.

What Are Ecosystems?

Ecosystems are communities of living things and non-living components that intertwine and depend on each other to survive. When living things, like plants, animals, bacteria, and fungi, exist together in a particular environment with non-living parts such as soil, water, temperature, and even weather, the whole thing together is considered an ecosystem. Ecosystems in water are called marine ecosystems. They're found in rivers, lakes, ponds, swamps, and seas. On land, the ecosystems are called terrestrial. Ecosystems can be huge, like the sand dunes of the Sahara Desert or the canopy of the redwood forest. They can also be small, like a tiny tide pool or even a patch of soil under a rock. In an ecosystem, everything is connected.

A whale fall is an ecosystem. It exists on a seafloor without much else around. It is a source of food that invites organisms to come and thrive. Predators come to feed on the scavengers. Microbes come to live on the bodies of animals eating from the whale fall. Those organisms begin to interact and depend on each other. Soon food chains become food webs and energy flows through the system.

For as long as there have been whales, there have been whale falls, but they were not really recognized or understood by scientists until a deep-sea whale fall was discovered off California around 1987. New technology allowed exploration of the whale fall in a new light, and since then, so much has been revealed. Never-before-seen species like bone-eating snails, snotworms, and sulfur-munching bacteria thrive in a busy ecosystem that didn't exist until a whale fell.

It's a Phase

There are four phases of a whale fall ecosystem as different parts of the whale are gobbled up and different animals come in to feed—not only on the whale but on other animals eating the whale and the things they leave behind, like skin cells and waste matter. These phases don't have hard lines of separation. They overlap each other.

The first phase is the **mobile scavenger phase**. This is where most of the soft tissue is eaten by scavengers like sleeper sharks, hagfish, and rattails. This phase can last a few months to a few years, depending on the size of the whale, and is considered done when the bones of the whale have been stripped clean of flesh.

The second phase is called the **enrichment opportunist phase**. Many of the species in this phase are found only on whale falls. Over time huge populations of bone-sucking worms set up shop on the skeleton to pull out nutrients. Crabs, lobsters, clams, and snails troll the surrounding sediment and feed on the material for years.

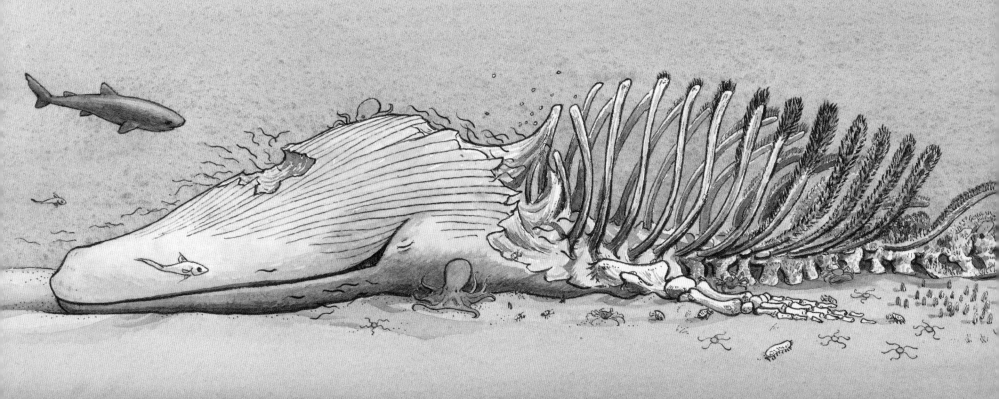

Specialized bacteria feed on the oils and chemicals deep within the bones and release hydrogen sulfide. This can be toxic to many life-forms but not at all toxic to the sulfur-loving organisms that move in during the third phase, the sulfophilic (sulfur-loving) phase.

Thick mats of bacteria devour the sulfur and turn these chemicals into energy. Other organisms flood in to feed on the bacteria that feed on the sulfur. This phase is the longest phase and can last fifty to seventy-five years.

In the middle of this sulfophilic phase is the reef phase. Large bones remain, taller than anything else on the surrounding seafloor. These bones act as a solid platform for new organisms to anchor themselves on as they feed on particles in the surrounding water. Anemones and sponges search the water for marine snow that drifts down from above.

Eventually the bone-sucking worms and the bacteria reduce the bones to a mere shadow on the seafloor.

A Little Pod of Whale Books

Hoyt, Erich, *Encyclopedia of Whales, Dolphins and Porpoises*, Firefly Books; Illustrated edition (September 1, 2017).

Carwardine, Mark, *Handbook of Whales, Dolphins, and Porpoises of the World,* Princeton University Press; Illustrated edition (February 25, 2020).

Skerry, Brian, *Secrets of the Whales*, National Geographic (April 6, 2021).

Whale Falls Online

Want to peek at a real whale fall? See the moment when scientists discovered a whale fall in the Monterey Bay National Marine Sanctuary off the coast of California at a depth of 10,623 feet. You can see octopuses, eelpouts, and crabs feeding on the carcass, and you can even see some worms feeding on the bones.
https://oceanservice.noaa.gov/facts/whale-fall.html

Take a dive and see some footage of whale fall phases at:
https://www.naturalworldfacts.com/whale-fall-ecosystems

Explore some weird worms that live on whale falls.
https://www.montereybayaquarium.org/animals/animals-a-to-z/whale-worm

Here's a beautiful and unique paper puppet version of life on a whale fall.
https://ocean.si.edu/ocean-life/marine-mammals/life-after-whale-whale-falls

Selected Bibliography

Fulton-Bennett, Kim. "Whale falls—islands of abundance and diversity in the sea." Monterey Bay Aquarium Research Institute, December 20, 2002.
www.mbari.org/whale-falls-islands-of-abundance-and-diversity-in-the-deep-sea/

Keen, Eric M. "Why Are Whales So Gigantic?" *Scientific American*, July 30, 2020.
www.scientificamerican.com/article/why-are-blue-whales-so-gigantic

Little, C.T.S. "The Prolific Afterlife of Whales." *Scientific American*, February 1, 2010.
https://www.scientificamerican.com/article/the-prolific-afterlife-of-whales

Smith, Craig R., Adrian G. Glover, Tina Treude, Nicholas D. Higgs, and Diva J. Amon. "Whale-Fall Ecosystems: Recent Insights into Ecology, Paleoecology, and Evolution," *Annual Review of Marine Science*, 2015. 7:571–96.

Smith, C.R. and A.R. Baco. "Ecology of whale falls at the deep-sea floor." *Oceanography and Marine Biology: An Annual Review*, 2003. 41, 311–354.

Acknowledgments

Because this is newish science, I did most of my research online and in specific interviews with the scientists who are doing the actual hands-on research. Dr. Craig Smith, currently a professor of oceanography at the University of Hawaii, was a fountain of information. He has spent a lifetime studying the ecology of the deep sea and is on the cutting edge of whale fall research. I learned so much by talking with him. Thank you, Dr. Craig Smith!

Also, thanks to senior research technician Shannon Johnson from the Monterey Bay Aquarium Research Institute, who clarified my understanding of bone-sucking worms and whale fall phases.

This book wouldn't have happened without the skilled guidance of the talented Neal Porter and the glorious artwork of Jason Chin, nor, for that matter, the gracious introductions and encouragements of Kelly Sonnack.

For my hero, Sir David Attenborough—curious, generous, brilliant and inspiring —L.B.

To Jennifer Lavonier —J.C.

Neal Porter Books

Text copyright © 2024 by Lynn Brunelle

Illustrations copyright © 2024 by Jason Chin

All Rights Reserved

HOLIDAY HOUSE is registered in the U.S. Patent and Trademark Office.

Printed and bound in February 2024 at Toppan Leefung, Dongguan, China.

The artwork for this book was created with with watercolor and gouache on paper.

Book design by Jennifer Browne

www.holidayhouse.com

First Edition

10 9 8 7 6 5 4 3 2 1

Library of Congress Cataloging-in-Publication Data

Names: Brunelle, Lynn, author. | Chin, Jason, 1978– illustrator.

Title: Life after whale : the amazing ecosystem of a whale fall / by Lynn Brunelle ; illustrated by Jason Chin.

Description: First edition. | New York : Holiday House, [2024] | Includes bibliographical references. | Audience: Ages 4 to 8 | Audience: Grades K-1 | Summary: "A book about the rich ecosystem that springs up around the death of a whale in the deep sea"— Provided by publisher.

Identifiers: LCCN 2022033729 | ISBN 9780823452286 (hardcover)

Subjects: LCSH: Deep-sea ecology—Juvenile literature. | Deep-sea animals—Food—Juvenile literature. | Whales—Juvenile literature.

Classification: LCC QH541.5.D35 B78 2024 | DDC 577.7/9—dc23/eng/20220831

LC record available at https://lccn.loc.gov/2022033729

ISBN: 978-0-8234-5228-6 (hardcover)